EXTREME SPORTS

SKYDIVING

by Tracy Vonder Brink

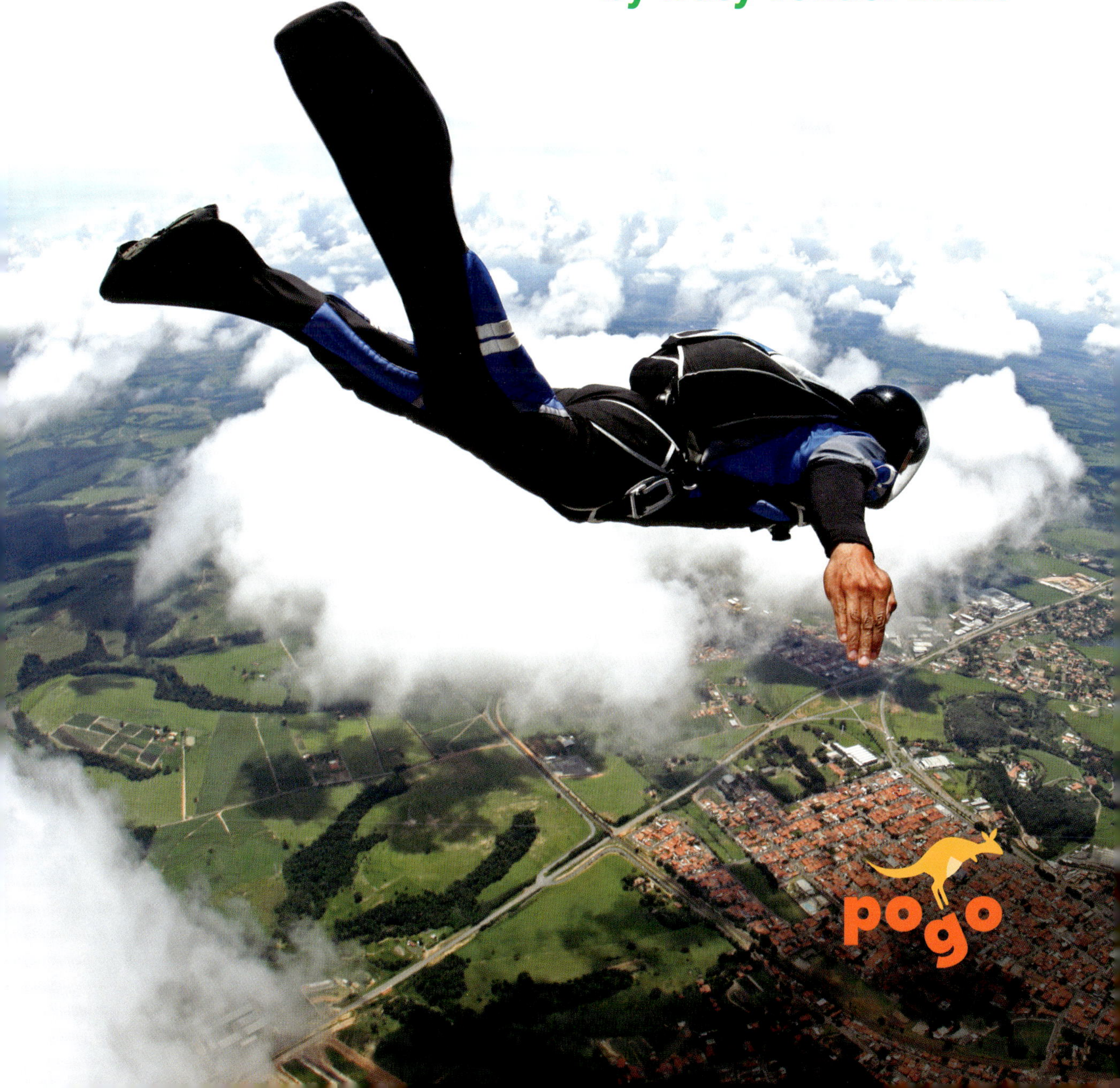

pogo

Ideas for Parents and Teachers

Pogo Books let children practice reading informational text while introducing them to nonfiction features such as headings, labels, sidebars, maps, and diagrams, as well as a table of contents, glossary, and index.

Carefully leveled text with a strong photo match offers early fluent readers the support they need to succeed.

Before Reading

- "Walk" through the book and point out the various nonfiction features. Ask the student what purpose each feature serves.
- Look at the glossary together. Read and discuss the words.

Read the Book

- Have the child read the book independently.
- Invite them to list questions that arise from reading.

After Reading

- Discuss the child's questions. Talk about how they might find answers to those questions.
- Prompt the child to think more. Ask: Would you like to skydive? Why or why not?

Pogo Books are published by Jump!
5357 Penn Avenue South
Minneapolis, MN 55419
www.jumplibrary.com

Copyright © 2025 Jump!
International copyright reserved in all countries.
No part of this book may be reproduced in any form without written permission from the publisher.

Library of Congress Cataloging-in-Publication Data

Names: Vonder Brink, Tracy, author.
Title: Skydiving / by Tracy Vonder Brink.
Description: Minneapolis, MN: Jump!, Inc., [2025]
Series: Extreme sports | Includes index.
Audience: Ages 7-10
Identifiers: LCCN 2024032964 (print)
LCCN 2024032965 (ebook)
ISBN 9798892136426 (hardcover)
ISBN 9798892136433 (paperback)
ISBN 9798892136440 (ebook)
Subjects: LCSH: Skydiving--Juvenile literature.
Classification: LCC GV770 .V66 2025 (print)
LCC GV770 (ebook)
DDC 797.5/6--dc23/eng/20240723
LC record available at https://lccn.loc.gov/2024032964
LC ebook record available at https://lccn.loc.gov/2024032965

Editor: Alyssa Sorenson
Designer: Molly Ballanger
Content Consultant: Jon Gleisner

Photo Credits: Sky Antonio/Shutterstock, cover, 8-9; Rick Neves/Shutterstock, 1, 17; Mauricio Graiki/Shutterstock, 3, 4, 6-7, 16, 18-19; Joggie Botma/Shutterstock, 5; Sanit Fuangnakhon/Shutterstock, 10; dzphotovideo/iStock, 11; Ensuper/Shutterstock, 12-13; ZhakYaroslavPhoto/iStock, 14-15; Sinesp/Shutterstock, 18; AscentXmedia/iStock, 20-21; Jarun Tedjaem/Shutterstock, 23.

Printed in the United States of America at Corporate Graphics in North Mankato, Minnesota.

TABLE OF CONTENTS

CHAPTER 1
Flying High 4

CHAPTER 2
Safe Landing 10

CHAPTER 3
Free Fall Fun 16

ACTIVITIES & TOOLS
Try This! 22
Glossary 23
Index 24
To Learn More 24

CHAPTER 1
FLYING HIGH

A small plane flies high in the sky. It reaches an **altitude** of 13,000 feet (3,960 meters). Skydivers leap out!

Gravity pulls a skydiver down. This pull makes them **accelerate**. They zoom toward the ground. At the same time, air pushes up against them. This causes **drag**.

CHAPTER 1

The skydiver falls belly-down. They arch their body. Why? It helps keep their **center of gravity** balanced. This keeps the skydiver steady.

CHAPTER 1

CHAPTER 1

They fall at a speed of 120 miles (193 kilometers) per hour. At this point, gravity's pull and drag's push balance each other. This is called terminal velocity. Skydivers still fall. But they no longer speed up. They fall at a **constant** speed. It feels like floating!

TAKE A LOOK!

How does terminal velocity work in skydiving? Take a look!

Gravity pulls the skydiver down.

Air pushes the skydiver up. This creates drag.

The forces of gravity and drag are equal. The skydiver falls at a steady speed.

CHAPTER 1

CHAPTER 2

SAFE LANDING

A skydiver **free falls** until they reach the right altitude. Then they open their parachute. The skydiver has to open it now. Why? It gives the parachute enough time to slow their fall. The drogue is small. It helps slow the fall.

altimeter

How does the skydiver know when to do this? They check an **altimeter**. It shows how high they are.

CHAPTER 2

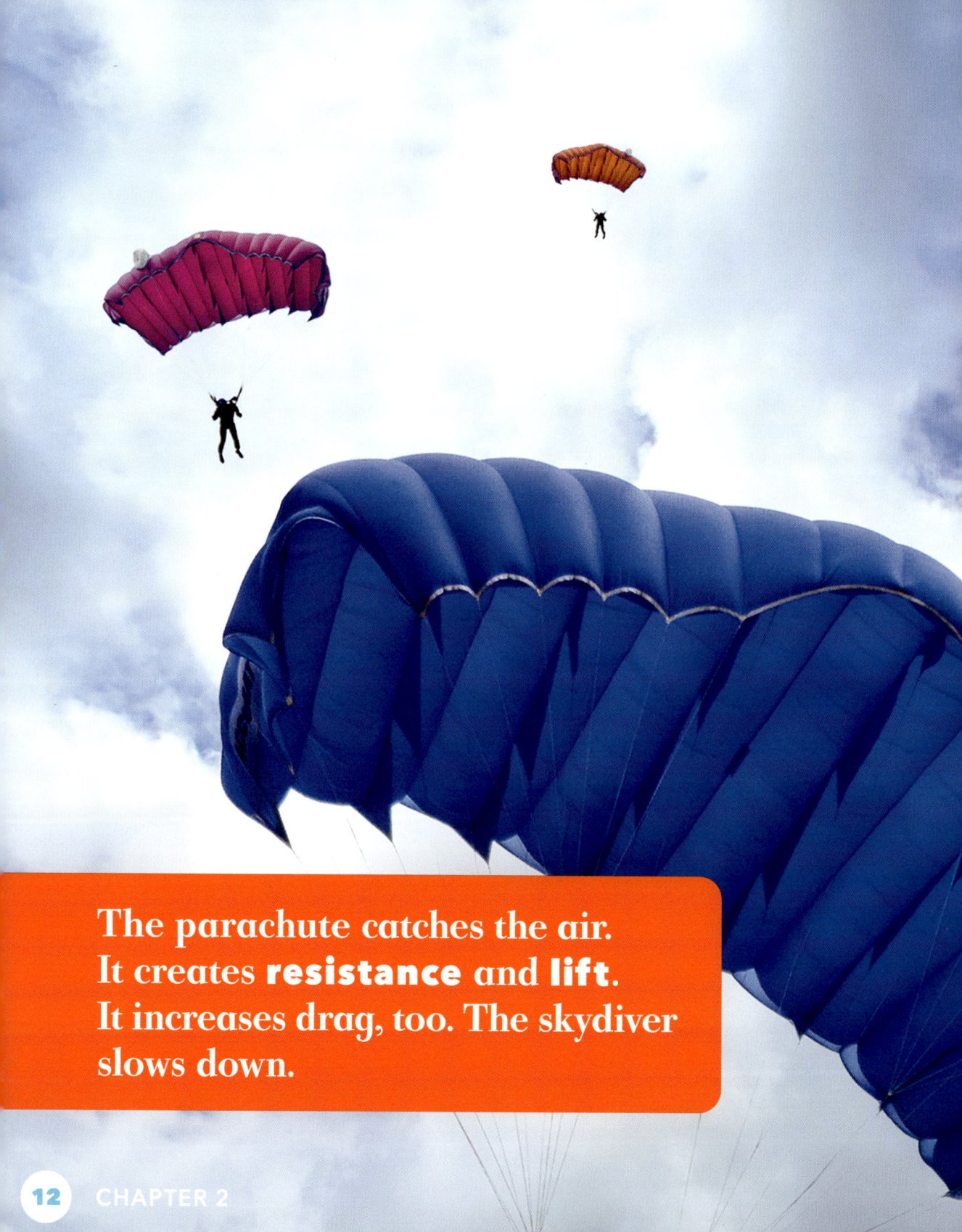

The parachute catches the air. It creates **resistance** and **lift**. It increases drag, too. The skydiver slows down.

CHAPTER 2

TAKE A LOOK!

What gear does a skydiver need? Take a look!

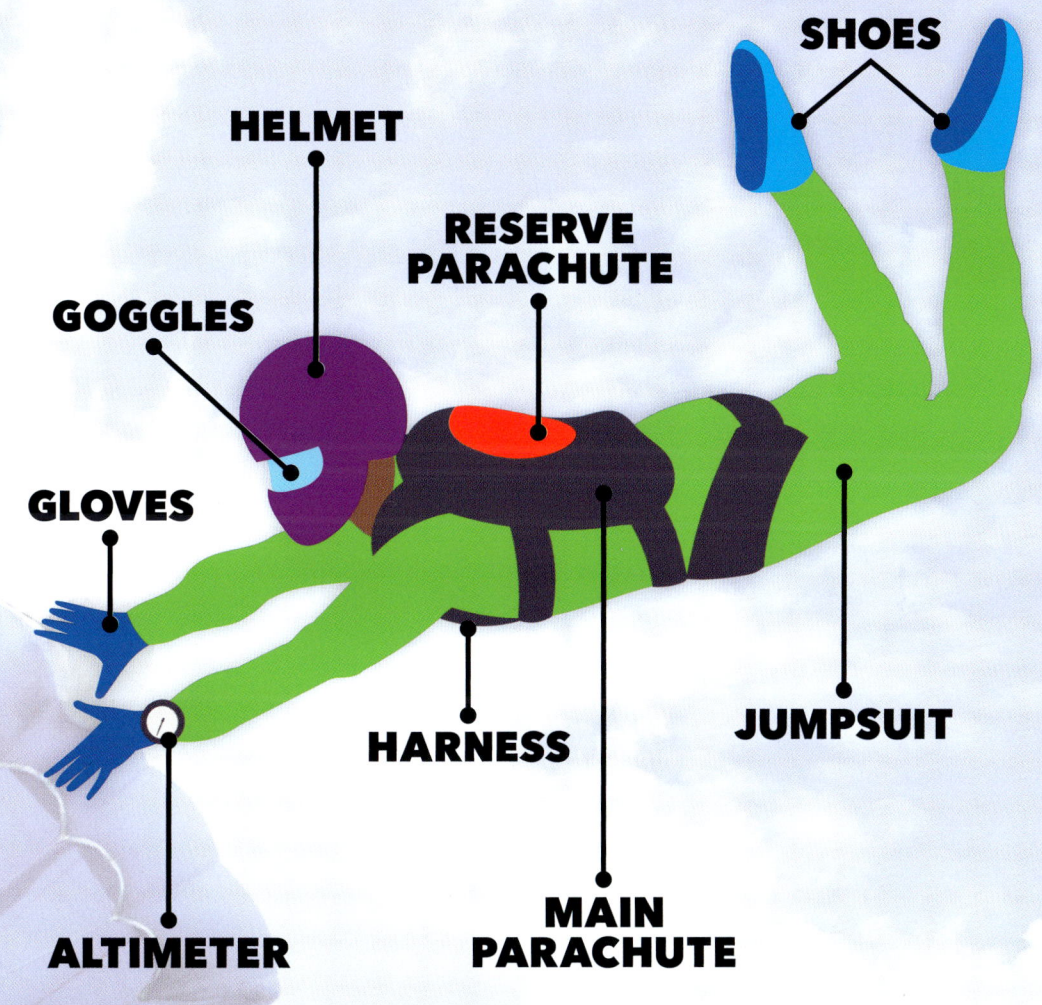

CHAPTER 2   13

The skydiver guides the parachute down. How? They pull handles. These are connected to **steering** lines. They turn the parachute where the skydiver wants to go. The skydiver keeps their knees and feet together. They land!

DID YOU KNOW?

Skydivers have a special name for a parachute. They call it a canopy.

CHAPTER 3
FREE FALL FUN

Skydivers use different body positions as they fall. Why? This changes the amount of drag. This makes them fall faster or slower. It helps them skydive in different ways. It is fun, too!

Speed skydivers jump headfirst. They hold their arms at their sides. This makes a **streamlined** shape. It helps them go fast. They can reach speeds of 330 miles (530 km) per hour!

CHAPTER 3 17

Some people wear wingsuits. This is another way to use lift and drag. As the skydiver falls, they hold out their arms and legs. This fills the suit's wings with air. It helps them **glide**.

Formation skydivers link up. They make patterns in the air. They hold each other's arms and legs to make shapes.

DID YOU KNOW?

As of 2024, the largest formation included 400 people!

wingsuit

CHAPTER 3

CHAPTER 3

The best skydivers **compete** in speed skydiving, wingsuit flying, and other events around the world. Understanding science helps them do their best!

DID YOU KNOW?

Freestyle skydiving looks like dancing in the air. Skydivers twist and bend their bodies.

CHAPTER 3

ACTIVITIES & TOOLS

> **TRY THIS!**

PARACHUTE TEST

Drag is the force that slows a falling parachute. Find out how it works with this fun activity!

What You Need:
- one single-ply square paper napkin
- four 10-inch (25-centimeter) pieces of string
- tape
- one paper clip

1. Tape one end of each string to a corner of the napkin.
2. Gather the free ends of the strings. Fold them together so they make a loop.
3. Wrap tape around the top of the loop to hold it in place.
4. Hook the paper clip through the loop.
5. Lift the parachute high. Let go.
6. What happens when you let go? What do you think would happen if you used something heavier than a paper clip?

GLOSSARY

accelerate: To go faster.

altimeter: An instrument that measures how high something is above the ground.

altitude: The height of something above the ground.

center of gravity: The point on an object at which half of its weight is on one side and half is on the other.

compete: To try to win a contest.

constant: Unchanging.

drag: The force that slows movement.

free falls: Falls because of gravity only.

glide: To fly without power.

gravity: The force that pulls things toward the center of Earth and keeps them from floating away.

lift: An upward force that opposes gravity's pull.

resistance: A force that opposes the motion of an object.

steering: Guiding or directing.

streamlined: Having a shape that passes easily through air.

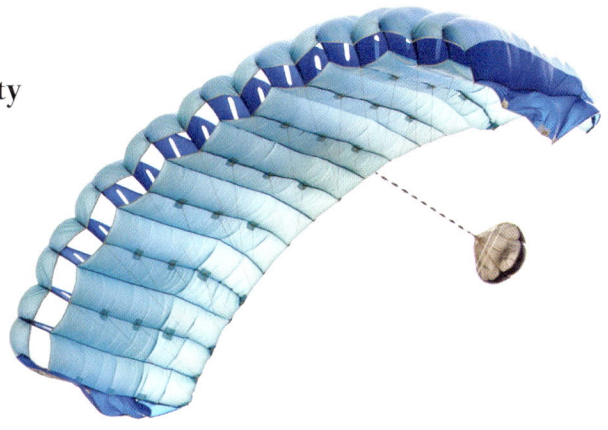

INDEX

accelerate 5
altimeter 11, 13
altitude 4, 10
canopy 15
center of gravity 6
drag 5, 8, 9, 12, 16, 18
drogue 10
formation skydivers 18
free falls 10
freestyle skydiving 21
glide 18
gravity 5, 8, 9
lift 12, 18
parachute 10, 12, 13, 15
plane 4
resistance 12
speed skydivers 17, 21
steering lines 15
terminal velocity 8, 9
wingsuits 18, 21

TO LEARN MORE

Finding more information is as easy as 1, 2, 3.

❶ Go to www.factsurfer.com
❷ Enter "skydiving" into the search box.
❸ Choose your book to see a list of websites.